KILLER
DINOSAURS

by Andrew Goldsmith

Consultant: Alison Howard

BEARPORT
PUBLISHING COMPANY, INC.

New York, New York

Picture credits(t=top; b=bottom; c=center; l=left; r=right): Fossil Finds: 7t,12t, 21t. Peter Griffiths: 9t. Luis Rey: 10-11c. Natural History Museum: 11t, 16-17c, 25t. Paul Sereno: 4l, 14b. Ticktock Media Ltd: 1, 2, 3-4c, 6-7c, 8-9c, 12-13c, 14-15c, 18-19 all, 20-21c, 22-23 all, 24-25c, 26-27 all.

Every effort has been made to trace the copyright holders, and we apologize in advance for any unintentional omissions. We would be pleased to insert the appropriate acknowledgments in any subsequent edition of this publication.

Library of Congress Cataloging-in-Publication Data
Goldsmith, Andrew, 1963-
  Killer dinosaurs / by Andrew Goldsmith.
      p. cm.—(Top 10s)
Includes index.
ISBN 1-59716-066-0 (lib. bdg.)—ISBN 1-59716-103-9 (pbk.)
1. Carnivora, Fossil—Juvenile literature. 2. Dinosaurs—Juvenile literature. I. Title. II. Series.

QE882.C15G65 2006
567.912—dc22

                              2005010284

For more information, write to Bearport Publishing Company, Inc., 101 Fifth Avenue, Suite 6R, New York, New York 10003. Printed in the United States of America.

                    1 2 3 4 5 6 7 8 9 10

CONTENTS

INTRODUCTION

Between 245 and 65 million years ago, thousands of different **dinosaurs** roamed Earth. Most dinosaurs were peaceful plant-eaters. Some, however, were ferocious, meat-eating **predators.** This book presents our Top 10 most dangerous dinosaurs. They were rated on a scale of one to ten in the following categories:

BODY MASS

Size was important for a meat-eating dinosaur. The bigger the dinosaur, the bigger the **prey** it could attack. A heavy dinosaur also found it easier to overpower its prey. We gave our dinosaurs a score based on their size and weight. We also considered the average size of their prey.

MOBILITY

High speed is important for a hunter. Yet, the ability to change direction easily and come to a quick stop is also important. Our dinosaur predators were given points for their speed, **acceleration**, and **agility**. Extra points were awarded for good jumping skills.

NO. 9 — VELOCIRAPTOR

Velociraptor had speed, power, and deadly teeth. Only its small size prevents it from being the overall winner of our Top 10 contest. Velociraptor lived in Asia towards the end of the Cretaceous period.

BODY MASS
Velociraptor was about the size of a turkey. It weighed between 44–55 pounds (20–25 kg).

JAW POWER
The dinosaur had about 80 teeth for ripping and tearing flesh. Narrow jaws allowed Velociraptor to push its head inside the **carcass** of its victim.

MOBILITY
Velociraptor was a fast bipedal dinosaur. Its name means "fast thief."

8

JAW POWER

Most dinosaur predators used their jaws for killing. We based our score on the size and strength of the jaws. We also took into account the number, length, and sharpness of the teeth. The few dinosaurs that also had deadly claws were awarded bonus points.

FRIGHT FACTOR

Some meat-eating dinosaurs were as big as a bus. Any predator that size is scary. Surprisingly, however, the largest dinosaurs were not always the most frightening.

Velociraptor fossils were discovered in 1924 in Mongolia by U.S. paleontologists.

Velociraptor was one of the fastest and fiercest predators that ever lived.

EXTREME SCORES

Velociraptor's small body keeps its scores low.

MOBILITY 10/10

BODY MASS 1/10

JAW POWER 2/10

FRIGHT FACTOR 1/10

HUNTING SKILLS 8/10

= TOTAL SCORE 22/50

FRIGHT FACTOR

A Velociraptor was not much larger that a pet cat. However, you wouldn't want to meet a pack of these fierce little dinosaurs.

HUNTING SKILLS

Velociraptor was a highly skilled predator that hunted in packs. It attacked with the claws of all four limbs. It could even jump up onto the back of its prey.

HUNTING SKILLS

Some dinosaurs hunted in **packs**, while others lived and hunted alone. Some dinosaurs waited in **ambush** for their prey. Others were constantly on the prowl for something to eat. We based our scores on the overall hunting technique.

Dilophosaurus lived during the early part of the **Jurassic period**. This flesh-eating dinosaur had a special **crest** along the top of its skull. Its **fossils** were discovered in 1942 in Arizona by the **paleontologist** Samuel Welles.

BODY MASS

Dilophosaurus was about 20 feet (6 m) in length. It weighed about 1,100 pounds (499 kg).

Dilophosaurus had an unusually long tail for an active predator.

MOBILITY

Dilophosaurus was a **bipedal** animal. It hunted by chasing its prey. Powerful muscles in the back legs helped it to run quickly.

JAW POWER

Although the dinosaur's jaws had long sharp teeth, they were fairly weak. Dilophosaurus must also have used its claws to attack its prey.

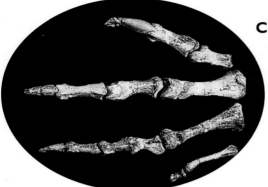

Claws at the ends of its fingers and toes were very sharp, but short.

FRIGHT FACTOR

Dilophosaurus was big enough to look scary. However, its jaws were not as strong as they looked.

HUNTING SKILLS

Most scientists believe that Dilophosaurus hunted in packs to help it attack animals much larger than itself. Other scientists, however, think that Dilophosaurus fed only on dead animals that it found.

Dilophosaurus just makes it into our Top 10 because of its high score for **mobility**.

MOBILITY
7/10

BODY MASS
3/10

JAW POWER
1/10

FRIGHT FACTOR
3/10

HUNTING SKILLS
4/10

= TOTAL SCORE

18/50

VELOCIRAPTOR

Velociraptor had speed, power, and deadly teeth. Only its small size prevents it from being the overall winner of our Top 10 contest. Velociraptor lived in Asia towards the end of the **Cretaceous period**.

BODY MASS

Velociraptor was about the size of a turkey. It weighed between 44–55 pounds (20–25 kg).

JAW POWER

The dinosaur had about 80 teeth for ripping and tearing flesh. Narrow jaws allowed Velociraptor to push its head inside the **carcass** of its victim.

MOBILITY

Velociraptor was a fast bipedal dinosaur. Its name means "fast thief."

Velociraptor fossils were discovered in 1924 in Mongolia by U.S. paleontologists.

Velociraptor was one of the fastest and fiercest predators that ever lived.

FRIGHT FACTOR

A Velociraptor was not much larger that a pet cat. However, you wouldn't want to meet a pack of these fierce little dinosaurs.

HUNTING SKILLS

Velociraptor was a highly skilled predator that hunted in packs. It attacked with the claws of all four limbs. It could even jump up onto the back of its prey.

EXTREME SCORES

Velociraptor's small body keeps its scores low.

MOBILITY
10 / 10

BODY MASS
1 / 10

JAW POWER
2 / 10

FRIGHT FACTOR
1 / 10

HUNTING SKILLS
8 / 10

= TOTAL SCORE
22 / 50

GIGANTOSAURUS

Gigantosaurus is the largest carnivore that ever walked on Earth. It is also one of the most mysterious meat-eating dinosaurs. It was not discovered until 1994. A fossil-hunter named Ruben Carolini made the discovery in Argentina, South America.

BODY MASS

Gigantosaurus is the largest flesh-eating dinosaur discovered so far. It was 52 feet (16 m) long and weighed about 17,600 pounds (8,000 kg).

JAW POWER

The dinosaur's jaws were crammed with narrow, pointed teeth that sliced through flesh. The biggest teeth were about 8 inches (20 cm) long.

MOBILITY

For such a large animal, Gigantosaurus was a fast runner. It reached speeds of up to 9 miles per hour (15 kph).

A huge 6-foot-long (2 m) skull housed a very small brain.

FRIGHT FACTOR

Gigantosaurus was huge and looked very scary. Luckily, it seems to have been a rare dinosaur.

HUNTING SKILLS

Gigantosaurus probably hunted alone. It charged at its prey with its jaws wide open. It attacked plant-eating dinosaurs that were more than 65 feet (20 m) long.

Gigantosaurus lived during the middle part of the Cretaceous period.

This flesh-eating dinosaur was too clumsy to make it into the number-one spot.

MOBILITY
1/10

BODY MASS
10/10

JAW POWER
5/10

FRIGHT FACTOR
6/10

HUNTING SKILLS
1/10

= TOTAL SCORE
23/50

Troodon was a small bipedal dinosaur. It lived at the very end of the Cretaceous period. Troodon fossils have been found in Canada and the western United States. U.S. paleontologist Joseph Leidy named the **species** in 1856.

BODY MASS

Troodon was about 7 feet (2 m) long.
It weighed between 88 and 110 pounds (40–50 kg).

JAW POWER

Troodon had up to 100 curved teeth in its mouth. Each tooth had a wide, jagged edge for slicing through flesh.

These curved teeth are responsible for the name *Troodon*, which means "wounding teeth."

MOBILITY

Long legs allowed Troodon to take very big steps. It was probably the fastest runner of all the dinosaurs.

The shape of Troodon's body was very similar to today's ostrich.

FRIGHT FACTOR

Troodon was too small to be scary during the day. It would be a different matter if it took you by surprise in the dark.

HUNTING SKILLS

The best hunters often have large, forward-facing eyes like Troodon. This dinosaur may have hunted small **mammals**. It probably hunted at night or at dawn.

EXTREME SCORES

Although very fast, Troodon was a lightweight dinosaur that was only scary at night.

MOBILITY
9/10

BODY MASS
2/10

JAW POWER
3/10

FRIGHT FACTOR
2/10

HUNTING SKILLS
9/10

= TOTAL SCORE
25/50

During the middle part of the **Cretaceous** period, this dinosaur was the top predator in North Africa. It had razor-sharp teeth. It was big enough to attack and kill the largest plant-eating dinosaurs. German paleontologists discovered Carcharodontosaurus in Morocco in 1925.

BODY MASS

Carcharodontosaurus grew up to 49 feet (15 m) in length (nearly as big as Gigantosaurus). It weighed more than 15,400 pounds (7,000 kg).

FRIGHT FACTOR

This powerful dinosaur was big and very fierce. However, it moved so slowly that many kinds of animals could outrun it.

JAW POWER

This meat-eater had wide, powerful jaws. Its sharp teeth could easily cut through the toughest skin.

MOBILITY

Carcharodontosaurus relied on power and weight rather than speed. It could not run very quickly.

Carcharodontosaurus had a giant and powerful skull, as shown here next to a human skull.

Carcharodontosaurus was a huge dinosaur with shark-like teeth.

This deadly hunter was able to kill the largest of dinosaurs.

MOBILITY
2/10

BODY MASS
9/10

JAW POWER
4/10

FRIGHT FACTOR
9/10

HUNTING SKILLS
2/10

= TOTAL SCORE
26/50

HUNTING SKILLS

Carcharodontosaurus killed prey that moved slowly. These dinosaurs were not very skilled hunters and probably hunted in groups. They may also have been **scavengers**.

Albertosaurus was a saw-toothed killer that hunted plant-eating dinosaurs. It lived in North America during the last part of the Cretaceous period. Geologist Joseph Tyrell discovered fossils of Albertosaurus in 1884 in Alberta, Canada.

BODY MASS

Albertosaurus measured more than 26 feet (8 m) in length. It weighed about 6,600 pounds (2,994 kg).

JAW POWER

Albertosaurus had a big head with large, powerful jaws. Its upper jaw had about 36 razor-sharp teeth. The lower jaw had about 30 teeth.

Albertosaurus used its tail for balance.

MOBILITY

This large bipedal dinosaur may have reached 19 miles per hour (31 kph) when running at top speed.

FRIGHT FACTOR

Albertosaurus was both large and fast.

This skull still has most of the teeth in place.

HUNTING SKILLS

Albertosaurus may not have been a very good hunter. Its eyes were positioned at the side of its head. Hunters see better when their eyes are at the front.

Albertosaurus was a big, fast killer. Some other dinosaurs, however, were bigger and faster.

MOBILITY
6/10

BODY MASS
5/10

JAW POWER
8/10

FRIGHT FACTOR
4/10

HUNTING SKILLS
5/10

= TOTAL SCORE
28/50

Allosaurus was once the largest predator on Earth. It lived at the end of the Jurassic period and the beginning of the Cretaceous period. Othniel C. Marsh discovered the first Allosaurus fossils in Wyoming in 1879.

BODY MASS

Allosaurus was about 39 feet (12 m) long when fully grown. It weighed more than 8,800 pounds (3,992 kg).

JAW POWER

Allosaurus had about 70 sharp teeth. Each one was up to 4 inches (10 cm) long. However, the teeth were fragile and broke off easily.

Allosaurus had no natural enemies.

MOBILITY

This bipedal carnivore may have had a top speed of about 12 miles per hour (19 kph). However, it couldn't run for long distances.

These massive jaws leave no doubt that Allosaurus was a deadly predator.

FRIGHT FACTOR

This dinosaur was even bigger and more aggressive than Albertosaurus.

HUNTING SKILLS

These dinosaurs may have hunted in packs. Allosaurus used the 6-inch (15-cm) claws on its front limbs to slash open its prey.

Allosaurus's slow speed and lack of **stamina** kept it from reaching the number-one spot.

MOBILITY
4/10

BODY MASS
6/10

JAW POWER
9/10

FRIGHT FACTOR
5/10

HUNTING SKILLS
7/10

= TOTAL SCORE
31/50

SPINOSAURUS

Spinosaurus was a fierce predator that lived in Africa during the late Cretaceous period. It had a strange series of 7-foot-tall (2 m) spines along its back. German paleontologist Ernst Stromer von Reichenbach discovered the first Spinosaurus fossil in Egypt in 1912.

Spinosaurus looked like a dragon in a fairy tale.

BODY MASS

Spinosaurus was one of the heaviest meat-eaters. It weighed up to 15,432 pounds (7,000 kg).

JAW POWER

This dinosaur had a long, narrow jaw lined with sharp, pointed teeth.

MOBILITY

Longer-than-usual front limbs suggest that Spinosaurus may have walked on all fours.

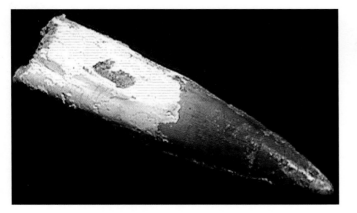

Each tooth was made to cut deeply into the prey's flesh.

HUNTING SKILLS

The design of its jaws and teeth suggest that Spinosaurus probably ate mostly fish.

FRIGHT FACTOR

This dinosaur is right out of your worst nightmare. It was a heavyweight killer with jaws like a crocodile.

Spinosaurus was large and fierce, for a fish-eater. However, it was a bit too slow to score any higher.

MOBILITY
5/10

BODY MASS
7/10

JAW POWER
6/10

FRIGHT FACTOR
8/10

HUNTING SKILLS
6/10

= TOTAL SCORE
32/50

Tyrannosaurus is the most famous of all the dinosaurs. It lived in the last part of the Cretaceous period. It's also one of the biggest land predators that ever walked the earth. It is often called Tyrannosaurus rex (or T. rex). *Rex* means "king" in the **Latin** language. Fossil-hunter Barnum Brown discovered the first T. rex fossils in 1908 in Montana.

BODY MASS

Tyrannosaurus was 39 feet (12 m) long. It weighed more than 15,400 pounds (6,985 kg). Its front limbs, however, were very small.

MOBILITY

This bipedal carnivore could run at speeds of up to 19 miles per hour (31 kph) for short distances.

This killer could tear off 441 pounds (200 kg) of flesh with a single bite.

JAW POWER

Tyrannosaurus had massive jaws with very powerful muscles. It could bite through even the biggest bones.

T. rex was part of a dinosaur family called tyrannosaurids. Three types are shown here.

FRIGHT FACTOR

The sight of this killer charging at you would probably frighten you to death.

HUNTING SKILLS

T. rex probably followed herds of plant-eating dinosaurs. It killed the weakest members of the herds—the very young and the very old.

EXTREME SCORES

This massive and terrifying killer had huge jaws and back limbs.

MOBILITY
3/10

BODY MASS
8/10

JAW POWER
10/10

FRIGHT FACTOR
10/10

HUNTING SKILLS
3/10

= TOTAL SCORE
34/50

DEINONYCHUS

Deinonychus was the supreme dinosaur predator—a fast and deadly hunter. It lived in North America during the early part of the Cretaceous period. Deinonychus was discovered in 1931 in Montana by fossil-hunter Barnum Brown. It was named in 1964 by U.S. paleontologist John Ostrom.

BODY MASS

Deinonychus was a medium-sized carnivore. It weighed about 176 pounds (80 kg) and stood 6 feet (2 m) tall.

JAW POWER

Deinonychus could bite off huge chunks of flesh. It had powerful jaw muscles and sharp, curved teeth.

MOBILITY

Deinonychus was a fast, agile predator. It could attack with the claws of all four limbs as well as its teeth.

Each tooth could cut through skin and muscle like the blade of a knife.

We call this dinosaur the fastest, and the fiercest. It was scary enough to give even a T. rex bad dreams.

MOBILITY
8/10

BODY MASS
4/10

JAW POWER
7/10

FRIGHT FACTOR
7/10

HUNTING SKILLS
10/10

= TOTAL SCORE

36/50

FRIGHT FACTOR

Just one of these dinosaurs was scary. No animal stood a chance against a whole pack of them.

Deinonychus was no taller than a person. Yet, it carried an incredible amount of killing power.

HUNTING SKILLS

The long, fierce claws on this animal's back limbs could rip open the largest prey.

CLOSE
BUT NOT CLOSE ENOUGH

Before deciding our Top 10 dinosaurs, we also considered these animals. All of them were deadly killers, but not quite deadly enough to make the Top 10.

HERRERASAURUS

Herrerasaurus was one of the very first meat-eating dinosaurs. It lived in South America about 225 million years ago during the **Triassic period**. Herrerasaurus was about 10 feet (3 m) long. It weighed about 220 pounds (100 kg). It walked and ran on its back legs. This dinosaur would have hunted small and medium-sized plant-eating dinosaurs.

COELOPHYSIS

Coelophysis was a fierce hunter that lived in North America during the late Triassic period. This small dinosaur was about 10 feet (3 m) long. However, it weighed just 55 pounds (25 kg). Hundreds of Coelophysis fossils were discovered at Ghost Ranch in New Mexico in the 1940s. The fossils revealed that Coelophysis sometimes ate its own kind.

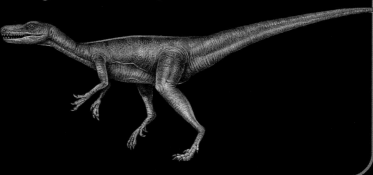

BARYONYX

Baryonyx was a slightly smaller relative of Spinosaurus. It lived in Europe and Africa about 120 million years ago. It measured about 33 feet (10 m) in length and weighed about 4,400 pounds (1,996 kg). Baryonyx probably hunted fish. It snatched them out of the water with its long jaws.

COMPSOGNATHUS

Compsognathus was one of the smallest-known dinosaurs. Its size, however, did not stop it from being an agile and efficient predator. This tiny animal was only about the size of a chicken. It lived during the middle of the Jurassic period. Compsognathus was bipedal. It used the claws on its forefeet to hold its prey. Then it bit off chunks of the animal's flesh.

STRUTHIOMIMUS

This fast dinosaur lived in North America about 75 million years ago. Its name means "ostrich mimic." Like today's ostrich, this dinosaur ate anything it could find. Struthiomimus had large eyes at the sides of its head. It was always on the alert for danger. When threatened by larger predators, Struthiomimus could run quickly. It reached speeds of up to 43 miles per hour (69 kph).

STATS

NO. 10 DILOPHOSAURUS

Extreme Scores

Mobility	7	
Body Mass	3	
Jaw Power	1	
Fright Factor	3	
Hunting Skills	4	

TOTAL SCORE

18 / 50

NO. 9 VELOCIRAPTOR

Extreme Scores

Mobility	10	
Body Mass	1	
Jaw Power	2	
Fright Factor	1	
Hunting Skills	8	

TOTAL SCORE

22 / 50

NO. 8 GIGANTOSAURUS

Extreme Scores

Mobility	1	
Body Mass	10	
Jaw Power	5	
Fright Factor	6	
Hunting Skills	1	

TOTAL SCORE

23 / 50

NO. 7 TROODON

Extreme Scores

Mobility	9	
Body Mass	2	
Jaw Power	3	
Fright Factor	2	
Hunting Skills	9	

TOTAL SCORE

25 / 50

NO. 6 CARCHARODONTOSAURUS

Extreme Scores

Mobility	2	
Body Mass	9	
Jaw Power	4	
Fright Factor	9	
Hunting Skills	2	

TOTAL SCORE

26 / 50

NO. 5 ALBERTOSAURUS

Extreme Scores

Mobility	6
Body Mass	5
Jaw Power	8
Fright Factor	4
Hunting Skills	5

TOTAL SCORE

28 / 50

NO. 4 ALLOSAURUS

Extreme Scores

Mobility	4
Body Mass	6
Jaw Power	9
Fright Factor	5
Hunting Skills	7

TOTAL SCORE

31 / 50

NO. 3 SPINOSAURUS

Extreme Scores

Mobility	5
Body Mass	7
Jaw Power	6
Fright Factor	8
Hunting Skills	6

TOTAL SCORE

32 / 50

NO. 2 TYRANNOSAURUS REX

Extreme Scores

Mobility	3
Body Mass	8
Jaw Power	10
Fright Factor	10
Hunting Skills	3

TOTAL SCORE

34 / 50

NO. 1 DEINONYCHUS

Extreme Scores

Mobility	8
Body Mass	4
Jaw Power	7
Fright Factor	7
Hunting Skills	10

TOTAL SCORE

36 / 50

GLOSSARY

acceleration (ak-*sel*-uh-RAY-shun) the act of getting faster and faster

agility (uh-JIL-uh-tee) the ability to move quickly and easily

ambush (AM-bush) to hide and then suddenly attack

bipedal (bye-PED-uhl) a two-footed animal

carcass (KAR-kuhss) the dead body of an animal

carnivore (KAR-nuh-*vor*) a meat-eating animal

crest (KREST) a ridge or tuft on the head of an animal

Cretaceous period (Kri-TAY-shuhs PIHR-ee-uhd) a time period from about 146 to 65 million years ago, at the end of which dinosaurs became extinct

dinosaurs (DYE-nuh-sorz) reptiles that lived on land over 60 million years ago, and then died out

fossils (FOSS-uhlz) the remains of plants or animals, such as bones, that have turned to rock, or imprints made by plants or animals, such as footprints, that are preserved in rock

geologist (jee-OL-uh-jist) a scientist who studies Earth's rocks and soil

Jurassic period (juh-RASS-ik PIHR-ee-uhd) a time period from about 208 to 146 million years ago, during which many dinosaurs lived

Latin (LAT-uhn) a language spoken in ancient Rome

mammals (MAM-uhlz) animals that are warm-blooded, nurse their young with milk, and have hair or fur on their skin

mobility (moh-BIL-uh-tee) ability to move

packs (PAKS) groups

paleontologist (*pale*-ee-uhn-TOL-uh-jist) a scientist who studies fossils

predators (PRED-uh-turz) animals that hunt other animals for food

prey (PRAY) an animal that is hunted or caught for food

scavengers (SKAV-uhn-jurz) animals that find food by searching for dead animals

species (SPEE-sheez) groups that animals or plants are divided into according to similar characteristics

stamina (STAM-uh-nuh) the strength and energy to do something over a long period of time

Triassic period (trye-ASS-ik PIHR-ee-uhd) a time period from about 248 to 208 million years ago

INDEX